Snow on Bare Dirt

poems by

Karen Lee Ramos

Finishing Line Press
Georgetown, Kentucky

Snow on Bare Dirt

For my children, Megan and Daniel,
the reasons behind every why
and to Michael with gratitude, always

ACKNOWLEDGMENTS

I gratefully acknowledge the following publications in which these poems
previously appeared:

Paterson Literary Review: "Just Another Word" and "Unexpected Mercy"
The Stillwater Review: "Mourning", "Numb" and "That Owl"
Paulinskill Poetry Project's Voices From Here 2: "Stolen Change"
New Jersey Bards Against Hunger: "Marsh House"

Publisher: Leah Huete de Maines
Editor: Christen Kincaid
Cover Art and Design: Megan Lee Ramos
Author Photo: Michael Ramos

Order online: www.finishinglinepress.com
also available on amazon.com

Author inquiries and mail orders:
Finishing Line Press
PO Box 1626
Georgetown, Kentucky 40324
USA

Contents

WITH GRATITUDE

I like that tree in my forest
even though it is cut
it can still be beautiful.

—*Daniel Ramos*
from his poem, "Epilog"

JUST ANOTHER WORD

At fourteen
I wanted to be Janis Joplin
to have that raspy voice
come out of my still smooth throat
thought
I already knew the blues
what it felt like
when somebody took
another little piece of my heart.

I wanted to hear those *windshield wipers*
slappin time
sitting in the cab of some truck
as I sang my way out
left my crappy little life behind.

Trying to get that voice
the one I thought I wanted
I smoked half a pack of cigarettes
the first time
I sang her songs
at what passed for a dive bar
in downtown suburbia.

I belted out
freedom was *just another word*
but I had no idea then
how much there could be
to lose
when you think you got nothin left.

SNOW DAY

I hiked into the woods with friends
spent the morning
trying to keep a fire going.
By noon the others gave up
I stayed
took too many swigs
from a bottle of Southern Comfort
thinking
it would keep me warm.

Just before dark
an old man walking his dog
found me lying on the trail
so covered with snow
he thought
I was dead.

When he brought me home
I couldn't walk up the icy steps.
My father watched me crawl
told the old man
go to hell
when he offered to help.

I woke the next day
shivering on the bedroom floor
still
in my wet clothes
hoping
I thanked that old man
for the rest of my life.

STOLEN CHANGE

She had nothing to do
on cold days
but look for unlocked cars
at the shuttered train station
hoping to steal change.

Sitting in a dull green Plymouth
smoking a cigarette out of the wind
she found keys
in the ashtray
like an offering.

Before long
she was orbiting the parking lot
trying not to ride the brakes.

Mistaking those keys
for providence
she headed out on the county road
no direction in mind
surprised
at how easy it was
to stay between the lines.

SAVED FOR GOOD

Every spring
the Dresden tea set
came out of the hutch.

My mother washed
each piece alone
in a towel-lined sink.

A wedding gift, never used
still cared for
long after divorce.

Passed down to me
now, I set the table
fill our cups to the brim.

A TERM OF ENDEARMENT

Every month
we made the two-hour drive
from Jersey to New York
to see a parade
of fertility doctors.

One morning
stuck in the Lincoln Tunnel
again
he reached for my hand.
I snapped
Stop being so fucking nice to me!

Without taking his eyes off the road
he replied, *Okay*
Bitch.
We burst out laughing
so hard we cried
that day you were conceived.

BOUNTY ENOUGH

The old apple tree lay flat
after an ice storm
we propped it up
heaped cold earth around the base
hoped
new roots might take hold.

That next summer
I nearly took my last breath
as my infant daughter drew her first
taken early
to save us both.

In autumn
we found
an apple in the tangled branches
it was a small harvest
but there was already bounty enough.

NOVA LULLABY

You are new
as morning light

in your small orbit
an entire galaxy swirls.

I will make a wish
whenever you fall.

Fire brought you
into this world, yet

for now, let dreams close
those moon-heavy eyes.

ANICCA
Pali word for the Buddhist concept of impermanence

A late-night tummy ache
nothing serious
yet I long to ease
this small suffering.

Caressing your belly
I whisper
this will go away soon
to reassure you

nothing is permanent
not what hurts
not this night I cling to
you curled in my arms.

SEA CHANGE

Snowmelt turns the yard
to mud
the well-worn path downhill
from back porch to woodshed
is a trickling creek.
The kids find bits of bark and sticks
to set adrift.

Little boats capsize
upon jetties of leaves
and stones
but one twig keeps going
it sails underneath the raised shed
and is washed away.

My daughter whispers
all gone now
the youngest cries
pease come back
I bring him inside to nurse
and find
a lump in my breast
no larger than a pebble.

BULLIED

I escaped recess
hiding in an empty supply closet
curled up on the cracked linoleum
with a book
safe
until the bell rang.

Today
walking down a hallway
at Sloan Kettering
I found myself facing a door
the word *SUPPLIES*
stenciled in gold on pale wood.

I reached
for that doorknob
cold metal in the palm of my hand
then let go

not
because I didn't want to hide
but because
there is nowhere
safe
from the bully picking on me now.

THE KINDNESS OF STRANGERS

The day before my mastectomy
a clerk from Admitting calls
confirming the time
I should arrive at the hospital.

Without thinking
I blurt out
what if I can't go through with it
how late can I cancel
without messing things up?

The clerk takes a deep breath
before saying
You can't mess anything up
Sweetheart, this is all about you now.

The next day
I am lying on a gurney
waiting.
A voice calls my name
through the cubicle curtain
it is the clerk
on her lunch break.

Minutes later
my husband holds my hand
as they wheel me down the hall.
When they tell him that is far enough
she stays with me
all the way to the operating room.

NUMB

the word
is undisturbed
by sharp consonants
with a soft hum
at the end
barely breathing
like grieving.

NECROSIS

Dark bloom of a bruise opens
to reveal the wound beneath.

When the weeping stops
budding flesh draws closed.

Once dreaded
you welcome the petal-pink scar.

RIPTIDE

The chemo nurse tells me
my heart is beating faster
than the human body can sustain
we need to stop it.
Syringe poised
she says
you will feel like you are dying
but I've got you.

I wonder what that means
until it happens.
Folding in on myself
I collapse as if under a wave
forceful enough
to pull me down
through the linoleum
to the hospital parking lot below.

Then the tide turns
surges back over the shoals
of my shoes
up through my limp body
unfurling
the sails of my eyes lift
her voice a searchlight
asking if I know my name.

Letting go of my wrist
she says
everything is normal
but I imagine the IV she runs
is a mooring line.

REAPER

My grandmother wove
crosses
from sheaves of wheat
tied them to fence posts
hoping
to distract ravenous birds
away from the harvest.

I gather amber strands
of hair
the morning after chemo
and listen
for crows.

MOURNING

Glass door thud
now a dove
bewildered, paces
asemic prints
in fresh snow
before taking flight.

Later, shoveling
the mate is uncovered
open wings
now stone
still
I look to the sky.
No one is watching.

NOW WHAT

I.

The doctor draws
a rough picture
bronchial trees
inside oval lungs
with a constellation
of suspicious asterisks.
My heart still
wishing hard
I keep breathing.

II.

My last MRI
No Evidence of Disease.
Outside the hospital
a swirling dance
purple sweetgum
leaves fall
on the sidewalk
a new galaxy
of bruised stars.

RETURN TO THE CAPE

We follow Route 6
past souvenir shops
and the Eastham windmill
reciting the names of roadside motels
like mileposts
Even'tide, Blue Dolphin, Captain's Quarters.

In the house
white sheets draped over furniture
are gathered up
to hang on the line
with the same clothespins
my grandmother pulled from her apron pocket
pinched between sun-browned fingers.

That first night
going out for ice cream
we walk across Cahoon Hollow Road
to wander the uneven rows
of the old Congregational Cemetery
cones dripping
we recite the carved names
of old friends
we've never met.

MARSH HOUSE
Lieutenant's Island, Wellfleet, Massachusetts

Trees take turns with the wind
as the tide comes in
two arms of saltwater embrace the island
touching at the narrow bridge.

Water flows through salt grasses
in a web of branching veins
that rise
until road and marsh become bay.

Birds arrive
geese and laughing gulls
the arrow of a heron
glides above the reunited inlet.

At low tide the moors empty again
the rutted road returns.
Combed with sunlight
damp grasses become golden.

I want to memorize these patterns
of wind and water and light
but all I can do is watch them
come and go

until the call of an unseen owl
ushers in twilight.

FACTS OF LIFE

On our walk
I tell you
about plants and animals
lifecycles and love.

We talk about the dead
mouse you found
how bodies
become earth.

I know my heart
will nourish the ground
you walk on
after I'm gone.

As you wander ahead
picking dandelions
I watch you
making wishes.

THAT OWL

That owl was back
but she wouldn't show her face
to me.
She perched in the hemlock
eyeing the squirrels' nest
even as she seemed to be watching
the western sky
turn from blue to apricot.

When the colors faded to dusk
her wings stretched out
like a wide shawl
down she swooped, low
before rising up past my view
where she vanished
in thrilling silence.

I watched the empty branch
rebound
from the weight
of a significant departure.

Last time I saw an owl
perch there
I'd fallen prey to other talons
my breast torn open
by the surgeon's knife.

Maybe this wasn't the same owl
tonight.
Perhaps mine watches
from somewhere else
gripping another branch
waiting
in the dark.

UNEXPECTED MERCY

Snow sifted over the rough ground
torn up
by the heavy machines
installing our new septic system.

I look at the yard and see
what is missing
the empty hollow
where an old apple tree stood
I was told the loss was unavoidable.

New tanks are buried
as I watch through the same window
where
after my mastectomy
I looked out at the tree
searched its branches
for green apples
while the visiting nurse changed the dressings.

I will never see that same view
out the window again.
Grass will grow back over the gouged earth
empty places
will be filled in
there will be unexpected mercies
like snow on bare dirt.

WITH GRATITUDE

As I write this, it has been 14 years with *No Evidence of Disease*. I am profoundly grateful for every single day with my beautiful family and for all my wonderful friends.

Love and appreciation to poets Anna Appel, Edytta Wojnar, Jeanne Fleming, Joan Page Durante, Mary Crosby, and Valerie Schermerhorn for their enduring friendships and vital critique.

Many heartfelt thanks to everyone at the Writers' Roundtable and Silconas Poetry Center of Newton, NJ. You have brought so much joy to our family and we are incredibly lucky to know you all.

Much love to three remarkable poets I deeply admire: Elaine Koplow, Adele Kenny and Maria Mazziotti Gillan. Thank you for your generous support, encouragement, and wisdom.

Thanks to Leah Madsen and Ringwood Manor Arts for offering me the opportunity to create *POETRY at the BARN*. To all the poets who have participated and helped our programming flourish: you inspire me in countless ways, thank you!

I am grateful to Finishing Line Press for making this book possible.

Karen Lee Ramos is from the beautiful Highlands Region of northern New Jersey. She and her family live in a little house by the woods with a sweet old dog and plenty of local wildlife.

Karen is the poetry director for Ringwood Manor Arts, located in the historic Carriage Barn Gallery of Ringwood State Park. As creator of the popular series, *POETRY at the BARN*, she hosts virtual and live poetry readings, leads writing sessions and coordinates literary events.

A New Jersey native, Karen is an active participant in the area's vibrant poetry community. Her poems have appeared in various publications such as *Paterson Literary Review, Exit 13 Magazine, The Stillwater Review,* and anthologies such as the Paulinskill Poetry Project's *Voices From Here 2* and *New Jersey Bards against Hunge*r. She is available for events, workshops and poetry readings. Please feel free to contact her through her website, KarenLeeRamos.com